SO GLAD WE'RE SISTERS

MARIANNE RICHMOND

Published by Sourcebooks, Inc.
P.O. Box 4410, Naperville, Illinois 60567–4410
(630) 961–3900
Fax: (630) 961–2168
www.sourcebooks.com

Printed and bound in China.
LEO 10 9 8 7 6 5 4 3 2 1

To:_____

From:_____

I'm so glad
we're sisters!

I feel like I have a
built-in best friend for life.

friend. Secret keeper.
Encourager. confidante.
Silly. listener. smiles &
ups. downs. always there
tears. always there
with a kind word to
say. Hug. Playmate.
adventurer. Gratitude

To say we go way back
pretty much sums it up.

From sharing the TV,

bathroom,

and clothing

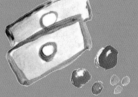

to negotiating chores...

and co-experiencing family
dinners, vacations, and chaos.

For as long as I can remember,
you were there.

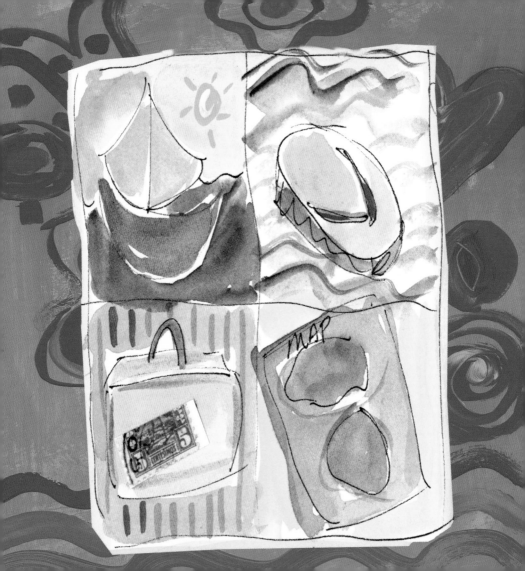

Oh, we've had some pretty good fights, haven't we?

Sometimes
I wasn't
sure we'd
ever forgive
each other.

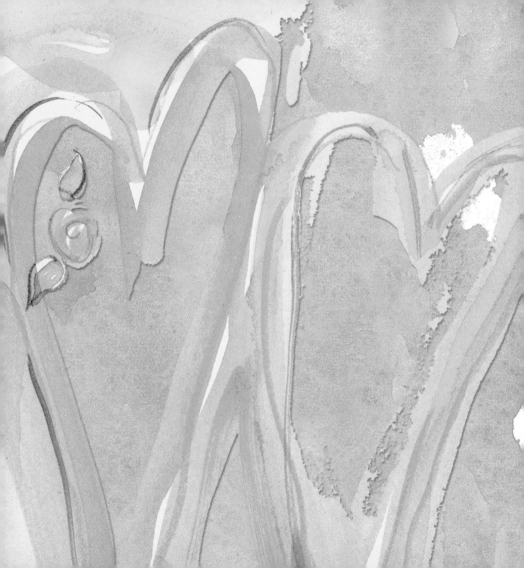

But we always did.

Until the next blowout.

I love how our
relationship grows and
changes with time.

Thank you for all the ways
you've been there for me.

Playmate,

teacher, confidant,

cheerleader,

and friend.

Publicist, therapist, and
defense attorney too.

I know my feelings
are safe with you.

I admire you.

Your spirit, strength,
and wisdom.

Your crazy sense
of humor.

Sometimes I wish I could
be more like you.

But then I'd miss out
on cherishing you
for who you are.

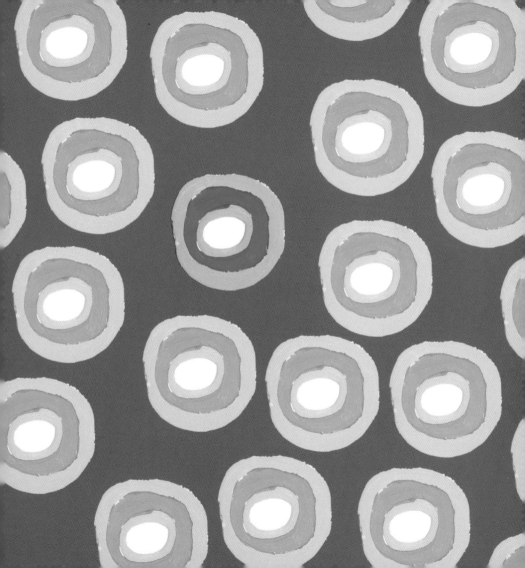

And how my life is enriched
because of you.

I love that we're family.

I love that we're connected.

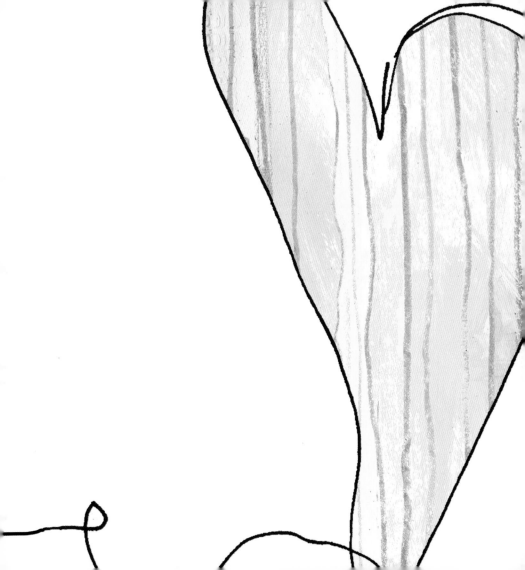

Thanks for listening
to me gripe.

And for loving me
through any mood.

I appreciate your advice.

Even though I occasionally
tell you otherwise.

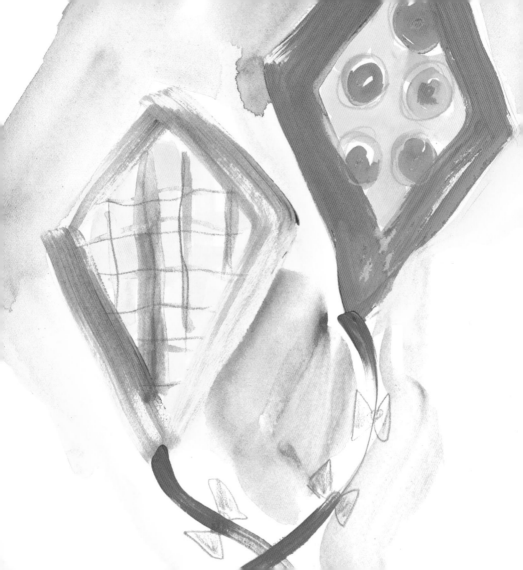

Thanks, sis, for making me laugh.

Sometimes so
hard I thought
I'd bust.

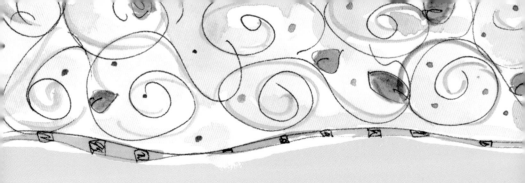

I love that you usually know

what I'm thinking.

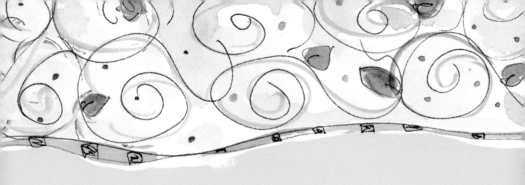

It's like we have this secret

connection that's ours alone.

You know me
like no other.

People will come and go in life.

They will be there for a
reason or a season.

But sisters are forever.

I'm so glad you're mine.

About the Author

Beloved author and illustrator Marianne Richmond has touched the lives of millions for nearly two decades through her award-winning books, greeting cards, and other gift products that offer people the most heartfelt way to connect with each other. She lives in Northern California. Visit www.mariannerichmond.com.